Holiday Baking PARTY!

Let's Bake
Valentine's Day Treats!

By Ruth Owen

Gareth Stevens
PUBLISHING

Please visit our website, **www.garethstevens.com**.
For a free color catalog of all our high-quality books,
call toll free 1-800-542-2595 or fax 1-877-542-2596.

Cataloging-in-Publication Data

Names: Owen, Ruth.
Title: Let's bake Valentine's Day treats! / Ruth Owen.
Description: New York : Gareth Stevens Publishing, 2018. | Series: Holiday baking party | Includes index.
Identifiers: LCCN ISBN 9781538213445 (pbk.) | ISBN 9781538213469 (library bound) | ISBN 9781538213452 (6 pack)
Subjects: LCSH: Valentine's Day cooking--Juvenile literature. | Desserts--Juvenile literature.
Classification: LCC TX739.2.V34 O94 2018 | DDC 641.5'68--dc23

Published in 2018 by
Gareth Stevens Publishing
111 East 14th Street, Suite 349
New York, NY 10003

Produced for Gareth Stevens Publishing by Ruby Tuesday Books Ltd
Designers: Tammy West and Emma Randall

Photo Credits: Courtesy of Ruby Tuesday Books and Shutterstock.

Printed in the United States of America

CPSIA compliance information: Batch CW18GS: For further information contact
Gareth Stevens, New York, New York at 1-800-542-2595.

Contents

Let's Get Baking!......................................4

Love Bug Cookies 6

Rainbow Heart Cupcakes 10

Strawberry Cream Tea...........................14

Chocolate Strawberry Cupcakes 18

Gingerbread Valentines.........................22

Raspberry Ripple Meringues....................26

Glossary...30

Index, Further Information.......................32

Let's Get Baking!

The most romantic day of the year is almost here. So it's time for you and your friends to show all your favorite people how much they mean to you by baking some delicious Valentine's Day treats.

Invite your friends to a holiday baking party and get started!

Get Ready to Bake

- Before cooking, always wash your hands well with soap and hot water.
- Make sure the kitchen countertop and all your equipment is clean.
- Read the recipe carefully before you start cooking. If you don't understand a step, ask an adult to help you.
- Gather together all the ingredients and equipment you will need. Baking is more fun when you're prepared!

Measuring Counts

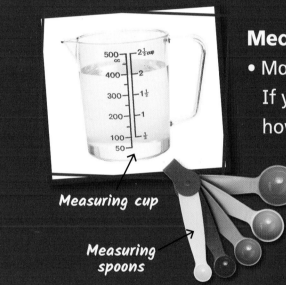

Measuring cup

Measuring spoons

- Make sure you measure your ingredients carefully. If you get a measurement wrong, it could affect how successful your baking is.
  - Use measuring scales or a measuring cup to measure dry and liquid ingredients.
  - Measuring spoons can be used to measure small amounts of ingredients.

Have Fun, Stay Safe!

It's very important to have an adult around whenever you do any of the following tasks in the kitchen:

- Using a mixer, the stovetop burners, or an oven.
- Using sharp utensils, such as knives and vegetable peelers or corers.
- Working with heated pans, pots, or baking sheets.

Oven mitts

Always use oven mitts when handling heated pans, pots, or baking sheets.

When you've finished baking, ALWAYS clean up the kitchen and put all your equipment away.

The quantities on this page will make about 25 cookies.

Ingredients:

To make the cookie dough:

- 1 ½ cups all-purpose flour (plus a little extra for dusting)
- ½ cup powdered sugar (plus a little extra for dusting)
- 5 ounces butter or margarine (plus a little for greasing)

For the frosting:

- ½ pound (0.5 kg) of red fondant
- Tube of black frosting (with a nozzle for piping)
- Ice cream sprinkles to make the bugs' eyes

Equipment:

- 2 large cookie sheets
- Mixing bowl
- Spoon for mixing
- Plastic wrap
- Rolling pin
- Heart-shaped cookie cutter
- Oven mitt
- Wire rack for cooling

Love Bug Cookies

These adorable ladybug cookies will make perfect Valentine's Day gifts for everyone you love! Get together with your best friends to bake a batch of these cookies and wow all your favorite people with love bug cookies on February 14.

Step 1
Grease the cookie sheets with a little butter to keep your cookies from sticking to the sheets.

Step 2
Put the butter and sugar into the mixing bowl and **cream together** with a spoon until smooth and fluffy.

Step 3
Add the flour and **beat** the mixture with a spoon until the ingredients are blended and become crumbly. Next, use your hands to squeeze and **knead** the mixture to make a ball of soft dough.

Step 4
Wrap the dough in plastic wrap and place in a refrigerator for 30 minutes.

Step 5
Preheat the oven to 350°F (180°C).

Step 6
Dust your countertop with a little flour. Unwrap the dough and place on the dusted surface. Roll out the dough to about ¼ inch (0.5 cm) thick.

Step 7
Cut as many heart shapes as you can from the dough and place them on the cookie sheets.

Step 8
Bake the cookies for about 15 minutes, or until they are turning golden. Using an oven mitt, remove the cookies from the oven. Allow to cool for about 10 minutes, and then carefully place each cookie on a wire rack and allow to cool completely.

Step 9
Dust your countertop with a little powdered sugar. Take a small lump of red fondant and roll out to about ¼ inch (0.5 cm) thick.

Cut heart shapes from the frosting for each cookie.

Step 10
Place a heart shape on top of each cookie and smooth down the edges.

Step 11
Use black frosting to draw on the ladybug's head, a dividing line between its wings, and several black spots.

Use the sprinkles to complete each love bug with a pair of eyes.

Sprinkles

Your love bugs are ready to give to the important people in your life!

Ingredients:

To make the cupcake batter:
- 7 ounces butter or margarine
- 1 cup superfine sugar
- 2 cups cake flour
- 1 teaspoon baking powder
- ¼ teaspoon salt
- 3 large eggs
- ½ cup milk
- ½ teaspoon vanilla extract
- Pink food coloring (optional)

For the decorations and frosting:
- 2½ cups powdered sugar
- 1 cup butter (tightly packed)
- 4 tablespoons milk
- Your choice of food colorings and sprinkles

Equipment:
- 12-hole muffin pan
- 24 muffin cases
- Mixing bowl
- Wooden spoon
- Electric mixer (optional)
- 12 marbles
- Oven mitt
- Potholder
- Metal skewer
- Small serrated knife
- Small bowls (for mixing frosting)
- Spoons

Rainbow Heart Cupcakes

A brightly colored cupcake makes the perfect Valentine's gift. These cute heart-shaped cupcakes are smothered with colorful, sweet butter frosting and decorated with a rainbow of sprinkles. Frosting and decorating cupcakes is a great way to show off your creative side—so let's get baking!

Step 1
Preheat the oven to 350°F (180°C).

Step 2
Line the muffin pan with muffin cases.

Muffin pan

Muffin cases

Step 3
Put the butter and sugar into the mixing bowl and cream together with a wooden spoon until fluffy. If you wish, you can do this step with an electric mixer.

Step 4
Add the flour, baking powder, salt, eggs, milk, and vanilla extract to the bowl. Use a wooden spoon or electric mixer to beat the ingredients together until the mixture is thick and smooth.

Measuring cup of flour

If you wish to **tint** your cupcakes with pink food coloring, add it to your batter now.

step 5
Spoon the mixture into the muffin cases, dividing it equally.

Cupcake batter tinted with pink food coloring

Marble

Gently insert a marble alongside each muffin case. This will form a dent that will help make the tops of your hearts.

step 6
Bake the cakes for 20 minutes, or until they have risen above the edges of the muffin cases. To test if the cakes are baked, insert a metal skewer into one cake. If it comes out clean, the cakes are ready.

step 7
Set the muffin tin on a potholder and allow the cakes to cool completely. DO NOT touch the marbles, as they will be very hot!

step 8
When the cakes are completely cooled, remove them from their cases. Carefully slice off the top of each cake with a serrated knife.

Put each cake into a fresh muffin case.

Step 9
To make the frosting, mix the powdered sugar, butter, and milk together until thick and smooth.

Step 10
Divide the mixture between several small bowls. Carefully add drops of food coloring into the bowls, mixing to get the frosting colors you want.

Step 11
Spoon the frosting onto a cake and use the back of the spoon to spread it out. Create a small "tail" of frosting to form the bottom of the heart.

Step 12
Add the sprinkles, and your rainbow heart cupcakes are ready!

The quantities on this page will make 10 scones.

Ingredients:

- 1 cup dried cranberries (or other dried fruit)
- Orange juice
- 3½ cups cake flour (plus a little extra for dusting)
- 2 teaspoons baking powder
- 1 stick of butter (plus a little extra for greasing)
- 2 large eggs
- 5 tablespoons milk (plus a little extra for brushing)
- Pinch of salt
- 20 large strawberries
- Strawberry jam and clotted or whipped cream for serving

Equipment:

- Baking sheet
- 2 small bowls
- Mixing bowl
- Hand whisk
- Sieve
- Wooden spoon
- Rolling pin
- 3-inch (8-cm) round cookie cutter
- Brush
- Oven mitt
- Wire rack for cooling
- Knife and cutting board

Strawberry Cream Tea

A cream tea is a delicious, **traditional** treat that was invented in England. With fruit-packed scones, jam, cream, and fresh strawberries, it makes a perfect dish to serve on Valentine's Day. And after all, with its natural heart shape, what fruit says LOVE better than a strawberry?

Step 1
Preheat the oven to 400°F (200°C).

Step 2
Grease your baking sheet with a little butter to keep the scones from sticking.

Step 3
Put the cranberries into a small bowl and cover with orange juice to soak.

Dried cranberries

You can use any dried fruit. Cranberries will give the scones lots of red flecks for Valentine's Day.

Step 4
Put the flour, baking powder, and butter into a mixing bowl. Rub the mixture together with your fingers until it looks like breadcrumbs.

Step 5
In a small bowl, beat together the eggs and milk with a hand whisk.

Step 6
Use a sieve to drain the cranberries and then add them to the eggs and milk mixture. Add a pinch of salt.

Step 7
With your hands, make a small hole or well in the flour mixture and then pour the eggs, milk, and cranberries into the well. Stir well until all the ingredients are combined. As the mixture gets stiffer, use your hands to create a ball of dough.

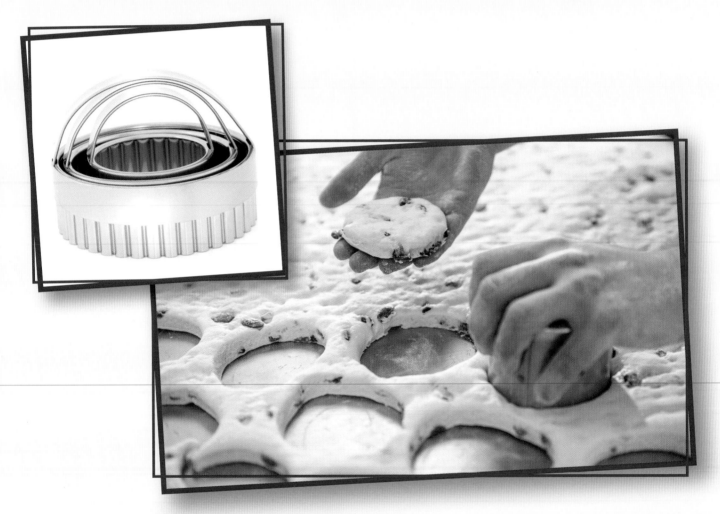

Step 8
Dust your work surface with a little flour. Roll out the dough to about 1 inch (2.5 cm) thick.

Step 9
Cut 10 circles from the dough with a cookie cutter and lay them on the baking sheet.

step 10
Brush a little milk over the dough circles. This will help give your scones a shiny, brown top.

step 11
Bake the scones for about 15 minutes, or until they have risen and are golden brown on top. Remove from the oven and allow to cool on a wire rack.

step 12
Wash the strawberries and remove their stalks and leaves. Carefully cut each strawberry in half.

step 13
To serve a scone, cut it in half. Add a thick layer of strawberry jam and cream, and then decorate with the strawberry halves.

The quantities on this page will make 12 cupcakes.

Ingredients:

To make the cupcake batter:
- 7 ounces butter or margarine
- 1 cup superfine sugar
- 2 cups cake flour
- 1 teaspoon baking powder
- ¼ teaspoon salt
- 3 large eggs
- ½ cup milk
- ½ teaspoon vanilla extract

For the frosting and decoration:
- 1 cup washed, chopped strawberries
- 2½ cups powdered sugar
- 1 cup butter (tightly packed)
- 4 tablespoons milk
- Pink food coloring
- ⅓ cup chocolate chips
- 12 washed strawberries with leaves on top

Equipment:
- 12-hole muffin pan
- 12 muffin cases
- Mixing bowl
- Wooden spoon
- Electric mixer (optional)
- Oven mitt
- Potholder
- Metal skewer
- Wire rack
- Hand blender
- Bowl
- Spoon
- Small saucepan and heatproof bowl

Chocolate Strawberry Cupcakes

If you and your friends love cupcakes, this recipe is a must for your baking party. Each tempting cupcake is topped with thick, strawberry-flavored frosting and a fresh strawberry that's been dipped in chocolate. They may be simple to make, but they taste delicious and look super luxurious!

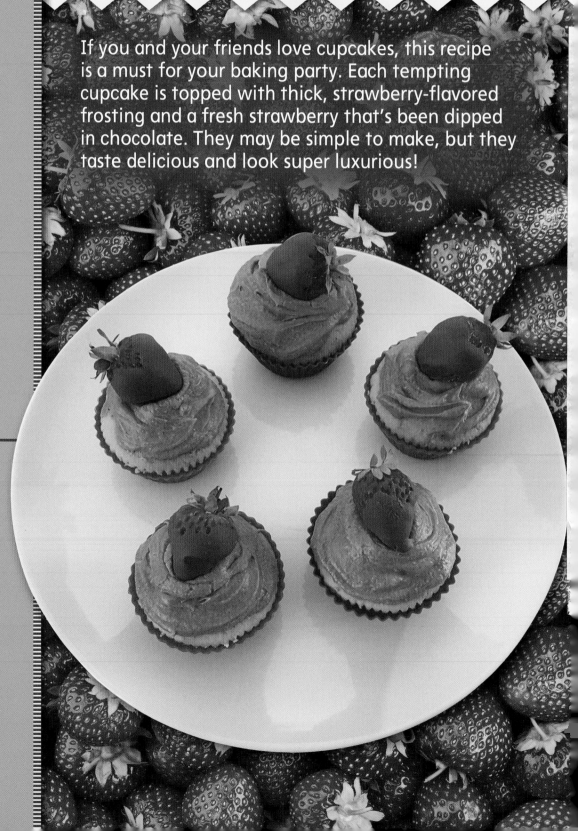

Step 1
Preheat the oven to 350°F (180°C).

Step 2
Line the muffin pan with muffin cases.

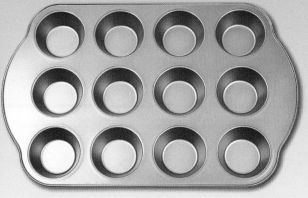

Step 3
Put the butter and sugar into the mixing bowl and cream together with a wooden spoon until fluffy. If you wish, you can use an electric mixer for this step.

Step 4
Add the flour, baking powder, salt, eggs, milk, and vanilla extract to the bowl. Use a wooden spoon or electric mixer to beat the ingredients together until the mixture is thick and smooth.

Step 5
Divide the mixture equally between the muffin cases.

Step 6

Bake the cakes for 20 minutes, or until they are golden brown and have risen above the edges of the muffin cases. To test if the cakes are baked, insert a metal skewer into one cake. If it comes out clean, the cakes are ready.

Allow to cool completely on a wire rack before frosting.

Step 7

With a hand blender, blend the chopped strawberries into a thick liquid, called a **purée**.

Strawberry purée

Hand blender

Step 8

Mix together the powdered sugar, butter, and milk until it is thick and smooth. Add about ¼ cup of the strawberry purée and mix thoroughly.

Add pink food coloring to the frosting, drop by drop, until you get the shade of pink you like.

If the mix is too stiff, add more purée. If it's a little runny, add more sugar, or put the frosting into the refrigerator to help it firm up.

Step 9

Put the chocolate chips into a heatproof bowl. Add about 1 inch (2.5 cm) of water to a saucepan and stand the bowl in the saucepan. Heat the saucepan on a medium heat, stirring the chocolate until it melts.

How to melt chocolate

Step 10

Dip a strawberry into the melted chocolate so it is about three-quarters covered. Place on a wire rack to cool and harden.

Step 11

To decorate the cupcakes, spoon a thick coating of strawberry frosting on top of each cake. Then add a chocolate-covered strawberry.

Happy Valentine's Day!

The quantities on this page will make 15 to 25 gingerbread people, depending on the size of your cutter.

Ingredients:

To make the gingerbread dough:

- 2¾ cups all-purpose flour
- ½ cup butter or margarine (tightly packed)
- Butter for greasing
- 1 cup light brown sugar
- 5½ teaspoons ground ginger
- 1½ teaspoons ground cinnamon
- 1 teaspoon baking soda
- 4 tablespoons golden syrup
- 1 egg
- Your choice of ready-to-use frosting or decorations

Equipment:

- Baking sheet
- Mixing bowl
- Wooden spoon
- Rolling pin
- Gingerbread man cutter
- Wooden skewers
- Oven mitt
- Potholder

Gingerbread Valentines

Spicy, **fragrant** gingerbread isn't just for Christmas. Make these cute gingerbread couples as a fun snack or gift for Valentine's Day. You can even turn them into fun lollipops by adding sticks. Decorate the cookies with hearts, flowers, kisses, or the names of any special couples that you know!

Step 1
Preheat the oven to 350°F (180°C).

Step 2
Grease the cookie sheet with a little butter to keep your gingerbread from sticking.

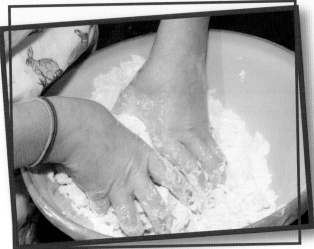

Step 3
Put the flour, butter, ginger, cinnamon, and baking soda into a mixing bowl. Mix and rub the ingredients with your fingers until they are crumbly and look like breadcrumbs.

Cinnamon

Ground ginger

Step 4
Add the sugar, syrup, and egg to the mixture. Stir the ingredients until they are well mixed and are binding together.

Use your hands to form the mixture into a ball of dough.

Step 5
Dust your countertop with flour and make sure your rolling pin is dusted, too.

Roll out the dough to about ¼ inch (0.5 cm) thick. The dough may be a little sticky, so keep dusting the countertop and rolling pin with flour.

Step 6
Use a gingerbread man cutter to cut out your people.

Cut two shapes and place them on the cookie sheet with their hands and feet overlapping. Press and squish the dough together to join the people and make a couple.

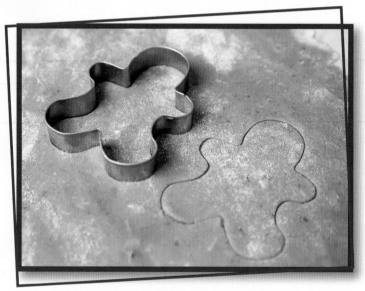

If you wish to make lollipops from your gingerbread Valentines, gently push a wooden skewer into each cookie.

Step 7

Bake for about 15 minutes. Test the cookies by gently pressing them. They should feel firm, but still slightly spongy.

Remove from the oven and leave to cool completely.
As they cool, the cookies will harden.

Step 8

Decorate your cookies with ready-to-use frosting pens or Valentine decorations.

The quantities on this page will make 15 meringues.

Ingredients:

- 1 cup washed raspberries
- 1 tablespoon powdered sugar
- 3 eggs
- 1 cup superfine sugar

Equipment:

- Jug or tall bowl
- Hand blender
- 2 small bowls
- Sieve
- Mixing bowl
- Electric mixer or whisk
- Baking sheet
- Baking parchment
- Spoon
- Wooden skewer

Crunchy and fruity — everyone will <3 them!

Raspberry Ripple Meringues

Meringues might seem complicated, but here's a secret—they are really easy to make! Impress your friends and family by baking delicious, sugary, homemade meringues with fresh raspberries swirled throughout them.

Step 1
Preheat the oven to 285°F (140°C).

Step 2
Cover a baking sheet with a layer of baking parchment.

Step 3
Begin by making the raspberry sauce, or purée. With a hand blender, blend the raspberries and powdered sugar into a thick liquid.

Step 4
Strain the raspberry purée through a sieve to remove the seeds. Set the strained purée to one side.

Step 5
To make meringue, you only use the egg whites.

Carefully break an egg on the side of a small bowl. Pull the shell apart as cleanly as possible along the crack, tipping the yolk into one half of the shell. Let the white of the egg drain into the bowl.

Do not allow any yolk to mix with the white.

Step 6

Pour the egg white into the mixing bowl. Repeat step 5 with the other two eggs.

Egg white   Egg yolks

If you break each egg into a small bowl first, you can start again without spoiling all the eggs if you accidentally split the yolk.

Save the yolks to make scrambled eggs.

Step 7

Use an electric mixer or whisk to whisk the egg whites. Keep whisking until they are thick, white, and stand up in small peaks.

Whisking egg whites

Peak of egg white

Step 8

Add one tablespoon of sugar to the egg whites and whisk for about 10 seconds. Keep adding the sugar spoon by spoon, whisking between each spoonful. The meringue mixture should look thick and glossy.

Step 9
To make each meringue, spoon a dollop of mixture onto the baking sheet. Swirl it a little with the spoon.

Step 10
Carefully **drizzle** a little purée onto each meringue and swirl with a skewer.

Step 11
Bake the meringues for one hour. The outside of each meringue will feel firm but in places may be slightly soft.

Step 12
Turn off the oven and leave to cool completely with the meringues inside. As they cool, the meringues will become crisp.

Glossary

beat
To blend a mixture of ingredients until they are smooth with equipment such as a spoon, fork, hand whisk, or electric mixer.

cream together
To beat butter or margarine, usually with sugar, to make it light and fluffy.

drizzle
To trickle a thin stream of liquid (such as runny frosting or purée) over food.

fragrant
Having a pleasant or sweet smell.

knead
To press, squeeze, and fold dough with your hands to make it smooth and stretchy.

preheat

To turn on an oven so it is at the correct temperature for cooking a particular dish before the food is placed inside.

purée

A thick, smooth liquid made from crushed or blended fruits or vegetables.

tint

Give something a color by adding a substance such as a dye or food coloring.

traditional

Something that has been a custom, belief, or practice for a long time and has been passed on from one generation to the next.

Index

C
chocolate strawberry
   cupcakes, 18–19, 20–21

F
frosting & decorating, 8–9,
   13, 20–21, 25

G
gingerbread Valentines,
   22–23, 24–25

H
hygiene, 5

L
love bug cookies, 6–7, 8–9

M
measuring, 5

R
rainbow heart cupcakes,
   10–11, 12–13
raspberry ripple meringues,
   26–27, 28–29

S
safety, 5
strawberry cream teas,
   14–15, 16–17

Further Information

Price, Pamela. *Cool Holiday Treats: Easy Recipes for Kids to Bake.*
ABDO Publishing Company, 2010.

Learn more about Valentine's Day here!
www.dkfindout.com/us/more-find-out/festivals-and-holidays/
valentines-day/

Publisher's note to educators and parents: Our editors have carefully reviewed this website to ensure that it is suitable for students. Many websites change frequently, however, and we cannot guarantee that a site's future contents will continue to meet our high standards of quality and educational value. Be advised that students should be closely supervised whenever they access the Internet.